This book is due for return on or before the last date shown below.

HEALTH AND SAFETY IN THE LIVE MUSIC AND EVENT TECHNICAL PRODUCTION INDUSTRY

A GUIDE FOR EMPLOYEES AND THE SELF-EMPLOYED

Chris Hannam

ENTERTAINMENT TECHNOLOGY PRESS

Safety Series

Kasabian at Victoria Park Leicester. Photo: Louise Stickland

HEALTH AND SAFETY IN THE LIVE MUSIC AND EVENT TECHNICAL PRODUCTION INDUSTRY

A GUIDE FOR EMPLOYEES AND THE SELF-EMPLOYED

Chris Hannam

Entertainment Technology Press

Health and Safety in the Live Music and Event Technical Production Industry

A Guide for Employees and the Self-Employed

© Chris Hannam

First published January 2015
Entertainment Technology Press Ltd
The Studio, High Green, Great Shelford, Cambridge CB22 5EG
Internet: www.etnow.com

ISBN 978 1 904031 80 2

A title within the
Entertainment Technology Press Safety Series
Series editor: John Offord

CODE / HSLMETPI001_01-15

CONTENTS

ACKNOWLEDGEMENTS

This book contains public sector information published by the Health and Safety Executive and licensed under the Open Government Licence.

Many thanks to Lansford Access Ltd for supplying equipment images.

Introduction

Health and Safety is a term that now crops up in just about every conversation about event and tour production; everyone has a major part to play in the process and it is essential that the new recruit understands his part in this process. The industry is also made up of hundreds of freelancers who ply their trade to the artists, production management and service companies within the industry and who need a means of proving they have received basic safety awareness training as they travel from job to job so there are various safety passport schemes in existence to provide exactly the kind of training that should be considered essential for everyone, this booklet mirrors the syllabuses and supports these schemes. The title has been written in good faith to help improve working practices and safety standards in the Technical Production sector of the live events industry. It is also designed to encourage and promote a positive safety culture. A safety culture is a term best used to describe the way in which safety is managed in the workplace, and often reflects "the attitudes, beliefs, perceptions and values that employees share in relation to safety". Unfortunately the culture is sadly missing in some parts of our industry and we are often left with a risk-taking culture.

The book is for guidance and the examples do not cover every situation, so please use common sense when reading, interpreting and following the information contained here, which is no substitute for proper training, instruction and supervision that by law, employers are required to provide. As stated on the copyright page of the book, the Author cannot accept liability for injuries to persons or damage to property or breaches of legislation by anyone using the information contained herein.

Health and Safety legislation is usually up-dated twice a year and everyone needs to keep up-to-date with these changes.

In this document the term "site" is used as a generic term to include all workplaces including venues both indoor and outdoor, offices, warehouses and workshops and the term "employee" includes the self-employed who are also known as freelancers.

We often hear of inconsistencies in Health and Safety standards and enforcement between one venue and the next. In our experience the only inconsistencies that exist are that some venues, promoters or employers enforce the regulations (to various degrees) and some don't.

Health and Safety law is implicit. We should not need others to "police" how we work and tell us when to use PPE etc. Sadly we don't have a good track record in this department and many people can't be relied upon to do things correctly themselves – so now, unfortunately, we can't be trusted to operate safely without being monitored and "policed". If you don't agree with me then I'd love to be proved wrong!

We often see uninformed statements in the press such as "elf and safety bans conkers" or bonfires and other activities. In truth, Health and Safety law hardly ever bans anything with the odd exception such as asbestos. It's usually an idiot who is interpreting the law wrongly, is introducing his or her own safety rules, or is using Health and Safety as an excuse for not doing something they can or should have done. Those to blame for making Health and Safety difficult are these idiots and the "no win, no fee" solicitors who make insurance companies twitch in an alarming manner. The result is, they start introducing stupid rules that have nothing to do with Health and Safety law.

There does not need to be an accident for you to breach Health and Safety law. There are more than enough opportunities for things to go wrong in our industry – so don't put your self and others at risk from hazards or prosecution. This attitude can get you and your employer a bad reputation, may well invalidate any insurance, and may also lead to court cases, fines, imprisonment, a loss of business, money and even bankruptcy.

Under Common Law we all have a Duty of Care towards each other so we must have a positive and safe Health and Safety culture and not an unsafe and selfish attitude.

This book is just a simple introduction and gives the answers to the common questions asked by employees; it tries to avoid too much legal jargon and reference to regulations where possible.

Health and Safety Management

The main piece of legislation that governs Health and Safety in the UK is the Health and Safety at Work etc Act 1974. Under this Act of Parliament lies a vast array of regulations to cover just about every health and safety topic imaginable. One of the most important of these is the Management of Health and Safety at Work Regulations 1999, which makes it a legal requirement for employers to "manage" safety in a similar manner as you might manage the financial aspects of a business. So you should have an auditable safety management system in place that includes appointing competent persons to advise and assist in these duties in the same way as you would appoint an accountant to help and advise on financial matters.

Legal Duties of Employers and Employees

Employers are responsible for the health and safety of, and have a duty of care for, everyone affected by the business and its activities.

All employers, whatever the size of the business, must:

- make the workplace safe to include access and egress (they must ensure any site or venue where employees are sent to work is safe).
- prevent risks to health and safety to employees working at the business premises, from home, or at another site, visitors to the business premises such as customers or subcontractors, people at other premises where you're working, such as a venue or festival site, members of the public – even if they're outside the business premises and anyone affected by products and services you design, produce or supply.
- ensure that plant and machinery is safe to use, and that safe working practices are set up and followed.
- make sure that all materials are handled, stored and used safely.
- provide adequate first aid facilities for all employees including those working away from base such as in a venue or event site.
- tell you about any potential hazards from the work you do, chemicals and other substances used by the firm, and give you information, instructions, training and supervision as needed.
- display the approved "Health and Safety Law" poster required by the Health and Safety Information to Employees Regulations explaining to employees what they need to know about health and safety.
- set up emergency plans.
- make sure that ventilation, temperature, lighting, and toilet, washing and rest facilities all meet health, safety and welfare requirements.
- check that the right work equipment is provided and is properly used and regularly maintained.
- prevent or control exposure to substances that may damage your health.

- take precautions against the risks caused by flammable or explosive hazards, electrical equipment, noise and radiation.
- avoid potentially dangerous work involving manual handling and if it can't be avoided, take precautions to reduce the risk of injury.
- provide health surveillance as needed.
- provide protective clothing or equipment free of charge if risks can't be removed or adequately controlled by any other means.
- ensure that the right warning signs are provided and looked after.
- report certain accidents, injuries, diseases and dangerous occurrences to either the Health and Safety Executive (HSE) or the local authority, depending on the type of business
- provide Employers Liability Insurance to cover all employees.
- provide effective arrangements for planning, organising, controlling and monitoring safety.
- consult with employees or their health and safety reps on matters of health and safety.
- ensure employees understand and carry out their responsibilities for health and safety, such as following the safety rules the employer has set up.
- ensure they have a competent person to advise (the employer) on health and safety matters.
- produce a Health and Safety Policy (if they employ five or more persons including partners, directors, etc). This policy must be in writing and must be brought to the attention of employees and contractors.
- employers are required to conduct a thorough assessment of the risks the business faces, if they employ five or more persons including partners, directors, etc. This assessment must be in writing. Employees must be given a copy of the assessments for the operations they undertake. Risk is the chance, high or low, that someone or something could be harmed by a hazard. Hazard means anything that can cause harm, e.g. chemicals, electricity, a slippery floor, work at height.

Employees Duties

Employees MUST:

- Use any plant, equipment and PPE correctly,
  - in accordance with instructions provided.
- Inform their employer directly:

- of anything that may be dangerous
- of issues that may affect health and safety
- Observe requirements of risk assessments including the use of PPE.
- Report lost, damaged or worn out PPE so it can be immediately replaced.
- Protect themselves and others who may be affected by their actions.
- Not damage or interfere with anything provided in the interests of health and safety.
- Take part in the H&S process.
- Cooperate with their employer in the execution of his legal responsibilities.

Your rights as an employee to work in a safe and healthy environment are given to you by law, and generally can't be changed or removed by your employer. The most important rights are:

- to have a safe place of work, safe equipment and safe systems of work.
- as far as possible, to have any risks to your health and safety properly controlled.
- to be provided, free of charge, with any personal protective and safety equipment.
- if you have reasonable concerns about your safety, to stop work and leave your work area, without being disciplined.
- to get in touch with the Health and Safety Executive (HSE) or your local authority if your employer won't listen to your concerns, without being disciplined.
- to have rest breaks during the working day, to have time off from work during the working week, and to have annual paid holiday.
- to receive information, instruction training and supervision.

Self–Employed Duties

The self-employed have the duties of both and employer and an employee. This is because they employ themselves.

An event organiser or promoter will often have additional duties including the requirement to comply with any conditions that may be attached to a Premises License issued under the Licensing Act of 2003.

Safe Systems of Work (Risk Assessments, Method Statements and Permits to Work)

Risk Assessments

A Risk Assessment is a systematic method of looking at work activities, considering what could go wrong, and deciding on suitable control measures to prevent loss, damage or injury in the workplace. The Assessment should include the controls required to eliminate, reduce or minimise the risks.

Risk Assessments are a fundamental requirement for businesses. If an employer does not know, or appreciate where the risks are, they are putting themselves, employees and customers of the organisation in danger.

Employers must look at all work activities that could cause harm in order to decide whether they are doing enough to meet their legal obligations. This is a minimum requirement. If it is reasonably practicable to do so, employers should consider doing more than the legal minimum.

The aim should always be to reduce the risks as much as is 'reasonably practicable'.

'Reasonably practicable' is a legal term that means employers must balance the cost of steps that they could take to reduce a risk against the degree of risk presented.

When reckoning costs, the time, trouble and effort required should be included and not just the financial cost.

The results of risk assessments must be communicated to employees so they know the procedures that must be followed.

The steps to risk assessment are:

- Identify the hazards.
- Decide who might be harmed and how.
- Evaluate the risks and decide whether existing precautions are adequate or more should be done.
- Record the findings.
- Review your assessment from time to time and revise if required.

Method Statements

A work method statement, is a written "safe system of work", a document that details the way a work task or process is to be completed. The method statement should outline the hazards involved and include a step by step guide on how to do the job safely. The method statement must also detail which control measures have been introduced to ensure the safety of anyone who is affected by the task or process. Instructions provided in manuals, etc by manufactures are also method statements that should be available to you and followed.

Permits to Work

Where proposed work is identified as having a high risk, strict controls are required. The work must be carried out against previously agreed safety procedures, a 'permit-to-work' system. Permits to work are legal documents.

The permit-to-work is a documented procedure that authorises certain people to carry out specific work within a specified time frame at a specified place. It sets out the precautions required to complete the work safely, based on a risk assessment.

It describes what work will be done and how it will be done; the latter can be detailed in a 'method statement'.

The permit-to-work requires declarations from both the people authorising the work and those carrying out the work.

Permits to work are often required for hot work such as welding, disk cutting, work at height, work in confined spaces, live electrical work, use of certain chemicals, etc and are often a requirement at many venues. Always check.

Health and Safety Law poster

Instruction, Training, Information and Supervision

The Health and Safety at Work etc Act 1974 requires all employers to provide whatever information, instruction, training and supervision as is necessary to ensure, so far as is reasonably practicable, the health and safety at work of their employees. This includes displaying the current Health, Safety and Law poster where all employees can see it.

This is expanded by the Management of Health and Safety at Work Regulations 1999, which identify situations where health and safety training is particularly important, e.g. when people start work, on exposure to new or increased risks and where existing skills may have become rusty or need updating.

Employers must provide training during working hours and not at the expense of their employees. Special arrangements may be needed for part-timers or shift workers. The self-employed should arrange for, provide and pay for their own training.

On starting in a new job or work on a new or unfamiliar site or venue, employees and self-employed staff should go through a short induction process were they will be made aware of the following:

- Emergency Exits and Exit Routes.
- How to raise the alarm in an emergency.
- The position or Fire Fighting and First Aid Equipment.
- Locations of First Aiders.
- The Emergency Assembly Point.
- Welfare facilities (Toilets, Drinking Water, catering etc).
- Accident Reporting procedures.

If you are not made aware of this information, find out for yourself before it's too late!

You are expected to cooperate with this procedure. You may also be required to attend and take part in any safety meetings, updates and briefings.

As soon as possible after starting work all employees should undergo:

- Basic Fire Safety Training
- Manual Handling Training
- Basic Electrical Safety Training
- Noise at Work Training
- Information on Safety Signs

This is where Safety Passports come in, they prove the holder has already received such basic training and it does not need to be repeated.

A few employees should be selected to undergo:

- First Aid at Work Certificate course or Emergency First Aid at Work Certificate course.
- Fire Wardens Course.

The Working Environment

So that the work premises provide a safe and healthy place to work, your employer should:

- make sure that workplaces are properly ventilated, with clean and fresh air.
- keep temperatures at a comfortable level – a minimum of 13 degrees C where the work involves physical activity or 16 degrees C for 'sedentary' workplaces e.g. offices but there's no maximum limit.
- light premises so that employees can work and move about safely.
- keep the workplace and equipment clean.
- ensure that workrooms are big enough to allow easy movement with at least 11 cubic metres per person.
- provide workstations to suit the employees and the work.
- keep the workplace and equipment in good working order.
- make floors, walkways, stairs, roadways, etc safe to use.
- protect people from falling from height or into dangerous substances.
- store things so they are unlikely to fall and cause injuries.
- fit openable windows, doors and gates with safety devices if needed.
- provide suitable toilets, washing facilities and clean drinking water.
- if necessary, provide somewhere for employees to get changed and to store their own clothes.
- set aside areas for rest breaks and to eat meals.
- let employees take appropriate rest breaks and their correct holiday entitlement.
- make sure that employees who work alone, or off-site, can do so safely and healthily.

Some basic rules apply to all workplaces:

- Smoking is not allowed in any enclosed working area.
- Any spillages must be cleaned up immediately according to appropriate procedures.
- Waste materials and rubbish must be routinely removed and placed into bins or skips for disposal.
- All combustible materials must be disposed of according to appropriate procedures.

- All open pits, trenches, holes, etc must be covered when not in use and clearly marked using the appropriate warning signs.

- Leads and cables must be laid and suitable covered in a way so as not to prevent hazard.

- Chemical waste must not be discarded into sinks, toilets, streams or other water courses.

- Aerosols and chemical containers must be discarded according to the appropriate procedures, not into fires.

- Employees are advised to always wash their hands before eating and drinking.

- All employees shall immediately report any unsafe practices or conditions to their employer or relevant authority.

- The use of alcohol and recreational drugs is strictly prohibited. Any employee found to be consuming alcohol or recreational drugs may be LIABLE TO INSTANT DISMISSAL.

- Walkways, passageways steps and stages must be kept clear from obstructions at all times.

- If a walkway, passageway, steps or stage becomes wet it should be clearly marked with warning signs and / or covered with non-slip material.

- Trailing cables are a trip hazard and should not be left in any walk or passageway, remember external cable ramps are to protect cables from vehicles moving over them, they are known to create trip hazards for pedestrians, one company was in the process for being sued when a pedestrian slipped on a cable ramp; the case was finally settled out of court by the company's insurers. Indoor lightweight cable ramps are to protect pedestrians but are not big enough to accommodate large cables.

- The downstage edge of all stages must be clearly marked with a of two inch wide white strip of paint or white Gaffa tape; the Stage Manager should ensure this has been done.

- In areas of low lighting (stage and backstage areas) any change in the floor elevation of any walkway or passageway must be clearly marked (white paint or Gaffa tape), the Stage Manager should also ensure this has been done.

- Where a passageway is being used by any vehicles or other moving machinery an alternative

Caution
Trip
hazard

route should be used by pedestrians wherever possible. If no alternative route is possible the area should be clearly marked with warning signs and any additional precautions as may be required must be taken to ensure safety.

Safety Signs

Safety sings are used to reinforce the safety message; they are not a means of controlling risk in their own right. They are to warn of any remaining significant risk or to instruct employees of the measures they must take in relation to these risks after all other controls have been put in place. You have a legal obligation to obey safety signs.

Warning – advise of danger or hazard

Prohibition – tells you *what not to do*

Mandatory – tells you *what must be done*

Information – provides safe guidance

Fire equipment – where equipment is located

Safe Working Area

As part of a safe system of work, before starting any work operation a safe working area must be established to protect staff, other persons working on site, and members of the public.

A safe working area can be established by fencing, taping or marking off an area. Cones and barricades can be used in the street around the doors of vehicles being unloaded/loaded.

Hazard warning signs may need to be erected and if necessary stewards may be required to assist in keeping the area clear.

Stewards and security staff can be enlisted to assist you, they have a very difficult job to do so please help them as much as possible, be polite and courteous, make sure they can clearly see your pass (even if they have already seen it a dozen times – it's their job to check) don't abuse you position by attempting to bring unauthorised persons hazardous working areas such as back stage.

Personal Well Being

Staying fit and healthy for work is essential. Tiring, physical work means that regular meals, breaks and drinks (non alcoholic) are essential. Incorrect clothing can make work uncomfortable and possibly dangerous. There is no better cure for fatigue than rest: don't be tempted into using an "artificial lift".

Drink or drugs and the workplace are an extremely dangerous combination and you will rapidly find yourself out of work if you indulge. You may find you have long periods of down time; a visit to the pub between load-in and load-out is NOT a good idea. You will not be welcome when you return to work if you have been drinking. This it puts added pressure on your workmates if you cannot be replaced at short notice.

Stress is now becoming a major hazard, the causes are often from outside of the working environment such as relationships or family problems, depression or money problems or bereavement, alcohol or drugs but will affect you at all times, seek medical or specialist support if you feel stressed or have specific problems, your employer should also be able help or give some support if you talk it over with them.

You should advise you employer if you suffer from:

- Asthma
- Epilepsy,
- Heart Problems
- Diabetes
- Back Problems

Personal Protective Equipment (PPE)

Under the Personal Protective Equipment Regulations employers have a duty to provide PPE free of charge to employees when it is required.

Employees have a legal obligation to use all personal protective equipment provided to them in accordance with the training and instruction given to them regarding its use.

To not do so places you at risk, puts your employer at risk of prosecution, breaks venue rules and may invalidate any insurance that you, your employer and the venue holds.

Employees who have been provided with personal protective equipment must immediately report any loss of, damage or obvious defect in any equipment provided to their employer so it can be replaced.

P.P.E. is personal equipment and should not be shared to avoid the risk of infection from ear protectors, gloves, boots, helmets, etc. This is particularly important with fall arrest equipment such as harnesses; they should not be loaned to truck drivers, etc so they can access followspot positions, etc.

No person shall carry out a task or operation without the use of the appropriate P.P.E.

To prevent ambiguity this is interpreted as meaning the following:

Safety Footwear (Steel toe capped)
All staff involved with heavy manual handling, forklift truck and plant operating must wear these.

Site Safety Helmets (Hard Hats with or without peaks)
These must be worn by all staff at all times within designated hard hat areas and by those involved in fork-lift truck operations and plant operating.

High Visibility Tabards and Jackets
These must be worn at all times when working on site and in areas where vehicles and plant are being used. They will also be required when loading or unloading trucks on public roads.

Gloves
They are also required when handling chemicals (including diesel and hazardous substances or when any damage to the hands could occur.

Hearing Protection
Must be used when there is a danger to the ears from high volume sound or noise such as when operating a fork lift truck or from a PA system.

People with Brains usually want to protect them Use your P.P.E.

Eye Protection
This must be worn when there is a danger to the eyes from chippings, spray, sparks, chemical splashes or flying debris.

Fall Arrest Equipment and Climbers Helmets
Fall arrest harness, connectors, shock absorber, fall arrest lanyards must helmets must be used by all those involved with climbing operations.

P.P.E. must be worn in this area

We should be grown up enough to be trusted to use PPE when it is required but many like to break the rules and not bother, so many sites and venues have had to bring in their own rules regarding the use of PPE. Many insist it is worn at all times; this is to protect their insurance and

THIS PROTECTIVE EQUIPMENT

MUST BE WORN

IN THIS AREA

to comply with legal requirements. You have a duty to follow the rules of the site or venue where you are working. These take precedent over you company rules in this situation.

Manual Handling

More than a third of all injuries reported each year to the Health and Safety Executive and Local Authorities are caused by manual handling: "the transporting or supporting of loads by hand or by bodily force. Most of the reported accidents caused by back injury – though hands, arms and feet are vulnerable.

In 1995, an estimated average of 11 working days per sufferer was lost through musculoskeletal disorders affecting the back, caused by work.

Employers have a duty to assess the risks caused by manual handling and take action to prevent injury.

Following these simple steps will help protect the worker.

1. Wherever possible, lifting and moving of objects should always be done by mechanical devices rather than manual handling. The equipment used should be appropriate for the task at hand.

2. The load to be lifted or moved must be inspected for labels giving weight, contents and centre of gravity as well as sharp edges, slivers and wet or greasy patches.

3. When lifting or moving a load with sharp or splintered edges gloves must be worn. Gloves should be free from oil, grease or other agents, which might impair grip.

4. Protective footwear must be used when lifting any heavy load or a load that is capable of damaging the feet if dropped.

5. The route over which the load is to be lifted or moved should be inspected to ensure that it is free of obstructions or spillage which could cause tripping or spillage, are the truck doors open?

6. Employees should not attempt to lift or move a load, which is too heavy to manage comfortably.

7. Where team lifting or moving is necessary one person should act as co-ordinator, giving commands to lift, lower etc.

8. When lifting an object off the ground employees should assume a squatting position, keeping the back straight. The load should be lifted by straightening the knees, not the back. These steps should be reversed for lowering an object to the ground.

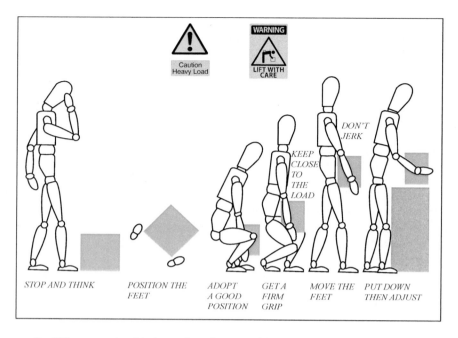

STOP AND THINK	*POSITION THE FEET*	*ADOPT A GOOD POSITION*	*GET A FIRM GRIP*	*MOVE THE FEET*	*PUT DOWN THEN ADJUST*

9. When carrying bin bags (e.g. litter) half fill them and carry them away from your body to avoid cuts and jabs; the bag may contain broken glass or other sharp objects. Always use gloves when handling litter and waste and wash your hands after work.

10. Always follow the training you have been given.

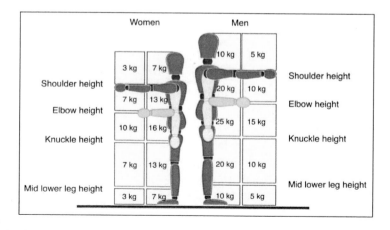

Electricity

Electricity causes shocks, fires, arcing and explosions. If you're not qualified as an electrician, don't tamper with it.

Electrical work must only be carried out by competent and qualified persons. Employers again have a duty to assess risks and give you a copy of the assessment so you know what controls to implement.

1. All portable electrical hand tools for use outdoors must be of the 110 volt (CET) type and protected with an RCD or better still, battery powered.

2. Employees shall not use their own electrical equipment unless it has been PAT Tested and permission obtained.

3. Beware of trailing leads that could be a trip hazard.

4. All electrical equipment must be given a visual inspection by the operator before use; this should include:

5. Looking to see that no bare wires are visible.

6. The outer case of the equipment is not damaged or loose and all screws are in place.

7. There are no taped or other non-standard joints (such a chocolate box connectors in the cable.

8. The cable covering is not damaged and is free from cuts and abrasions (apart from light scuffing).

9. The plug is in good condition, for example, the casing is not cracked, the pins are not bent and the key-way is not blocked with loose material.

10. The outer covering (sheath) of the cable is gripped where it enters the plug or the equipment.

11. The coloured insulation of the internal wires should not be visible.

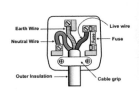

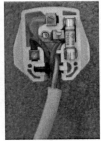

A correctly wired plug   *A badly wired plug*

12. There are no overheating or burn marks on the plug, cable or the equipment.

13. Testing trip devices (RCDs) regularly (i.e. monthly) to check they are functioning correctly by operating the test button this keeps the mechanical operation of the RCD free from sticking.

14. All electrical equipment is fitted with a fuse of the correct rating.

15. That is has been tested for electrical safety (Portable Appliance Tested) PAT

3 AMP	Up to 700 WATTS
5 AMP	Up to 1000 WATTS
13 AMP	Up to 1000+ WATTS

16. If a piece of equipment keeps "tripping out" an RCD or M.C.B, then that equipment should not be used until it has been checked and tested by a competent person and any fault corrected.

Apart from checking that a fuse of the correct rating is fitted there is little more a non-qualified person can do. Never try to remove or short circuit the trip; it is almost certainly your appliance that is at fault. Note: An M.C.B. (overload trip) is far less sensitive than an R.C.D. (earth leakage trip). An appliance well within the rating of an M.C.B. may well "trip out" if it has a fault when connected to a system with an R.C.D. The fault may not have shown up before if is had been used on a non-R.C.D. system, such as domestic installation that is not normally fitted with R.C.D. protection.

17. Any coiled mains lead will heat up in use. To prevent this, extension leads or reels should be fully unwound from their drums before use or they may heat up, melt together and cause a fire.

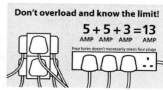

18. Multi-way blocks that allow more than one appliance to be run from one

Don't overload and know the limit!

$5 + 5 + 3 = 13$
AMP AMP AMP   AMP

Four holes doesn't necessarily mean four plugs

socket are a major danger. The rule is one appliance to one socket

19. Employees should report all faults and damage immediately and that piece of equipment taken out of service until it has been repaired.

20. Employees must be on the lookout for possible dangers such as damaged/faulty plugs and equipment, frayed cable, loose connections and poorly laid cables.

21. Checks must be made to see all connections are safe and tamper-proof.

22. All electrical connections must be made with the correct connectors and the correct gauges of cable. If in doubt, ask!

23. Never turn on the power to any equipment unless you have checked that it is safe to do so.

24. Employees must not touch or tamper with such connections unless they are qualified or have been given clear instruction about connecting and disconnecting and they are certain that the system is "dead" and therefore safe.

DANGER
Electric
shock risk

25. Always follow the manufacturer's instructions.

Work Equipment

Work equipment falls under the Provision and Use of Work Equipment Regulations and covers all tools and equipment used for work including vehicles, plant and machinery and rigging equipment.

Vehicles and Transport

Drivers must be suitable insured for the vehicle they are driving for work purposes.

All vehicles must be "Taxed" and hold a current MOT certificate – fully road legal.

Drivers are not permitted to drive under the influence of drugs.

Seat belts must be worn and it is the driver's responsibility to emphasise to all passengers that they are expected to use any seat belts provided.

Mobile phones must not be used by the driver while the vehicle is in motion.

Take adequate rest breaks and do not drive if tired and exhausted.

The speed limit for vehicles on outdoor event sites will be 5mph. All vehicles will keep to the agreed routes / roadways. Do not park in "fire lanes" and always park where requested, this may not be always where you want to park!

In the interests of fire safety, parking is usually prohibited in camping areas on outdoor sites.

No vehicles will be moved in the public areas of an outdoor event site once the gates are open to the public – without express permission.

It is the driver's responsibility to ensure that a pre-journey safety check is carried out on the vehicle; the following list is for guidance:

- Tyres appear road worthy, free of unusual signs of wear or low/high pressure.
- Vehicle body is in safe condition and no apparent fuel, oil or other fluid leaks.
- All loads are secure and not overhanging from the vehicle.
- All lights including warning /hazard lights are in working order.
- Oil and cooling system fluid levels.
- Driving mirrors are clean and suitably adjusted for the driver.
- Windscreens are clean and in good condition.
- Wipers are fully operational and wash bottles have a sufficient supply of liquid.

Additional rules may be applied for drivers of Company vehicles or vehicles on hire.

Hand and Power Tools

1. Many venues operate a Permit to Work system for certain work activities such as disk cutting, soldering, welding and live electrical work; always check before starting any of these activities.

2. Hand and power tools are only to be used by qualified and authorised personnel. It is the responsibility of your employer to determine who is authorised to use specific tools and equipment.

3. It is the responsibility of all employees to ensure that any vehicles, tools or equipment they use are in a good and safe condition.

4. Any broken, damaged or faulty work equipment (including electrical

equipment) must be clearly marked to indicate that it is non serviceable, taken out of service and reported to management so that it can be replaced or repaired.

5. All tools and equipment must be properly and safely stored when not in use.

6. Portable power tools for use outdoors must be of the 110 volt (CET) type and protected with an RCD or better still, battery powered.

7. No tool should be used without the manufacturers' recommended shields, guards or attachments.

8. Personal protective equipment such as boots, gloves, eye, face and hearing protection must be properly used where appropriate.

9. Persons using machine tools must not wear clothing, jewellery, laminate passes, wrist bands or long hair in such a way as might pose a risk to their or anyone else's safety.

10. Always follow the manufacturer's instructions and the training and information you have been given.

11. Always ensure you know how to turn off an item of machinery before you start it.

12. Approved personal protective equipment must be properly used where appropriate.

13. Employees are prohibited from using any tool, vehicles or piece of equipment for any purpose other than its intended purpose.

Plant

The basic categories of lift truck in normal use are:

- Rough Terrain Counterbalance Lift Truck
- Telescopic Materials Handlers
- Industrial Counterbalance Lift Truck

The basic categories of Mobile Elevating Work Platform (MEWP) in normal use are:

a. Boom type or Cherry Picker

b. Scissor type or Flying Carpet

- Forklift trucks and other items of plant must only be used by authorised personnel who are a minimum of 18 years old and hold the relevant national accredited and recognised certificate.

- Only authorised operators will be issued with keys. Keys must be removed and machines immobilised when left unattended.

- Under no circumstances will unauthorised persons operate lift trucks or plant.

- Operators will ensure capabilities of the machine are not exceeded.

- The plant **_must_** be inspected each day before use and the operator's inspection form must be filled in, any faults and defects must be reported immediately, the machine must not be used until all faults and defects have been rectified.

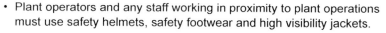

- Plant operators and any staff working in proximity to plant operations must use safety helmets, safety footwear and high visibility jackets.

- A "Safe Working Area" must always be established before work commences. Safety signage for plant workings must be erected and a speed limit of 5mph must be in force; areas where plant is reversing should must taped off if practicable and be clear of all unnecessary personnel.

- Passengers must never be carried on vehicles or plant not designed to carry passengers nor shall forklift trucks be used to lift people unless a correct and suitable "man cage platform" is fitted.

- All relevant plant must be inspected and tested on a regular basis by the approved contractor and must meet the requirements of the Lifting Operations and Lifting Equipment Regulations 1998 (LOLER) where applicable. The current LOLER test/inspection certificate must be provided for the machine by the hire company when it is hired, the certificate must remain with the machine. Operators must check this certificate is present together with the operator's manual before the machine is used.

- All overhead obstructions including power cables must be identified before work starts and clearly marked; where necessary they must be fenced or shrouded.
- Loading is only be permitted onto structures or vehicles designed to accept such loads.
- Access to all loading/off-loading points must be level, suitable and clear of obstructions.
- Mobile plant such as forklift trucks must not be used in public areas once the public have been admitted to the site/venue.
- Attention must be given to terrain, load requirements, reach, etc. when selecting lift trucks and plant for use.
- "Banks men" must be used when and where required.
- During refuelling and maintenance operations you must wear any required protective clothing or equipment such as gloves.
- The "flashing beacon" on lift trucks and plant must be used when the plant is in use.
- MEWPS must only be operated on firm level ground and any stabilisers fitted must be correctly used.
- Fall Arrest equipment must be used by operators of Boom Type (Cherry Picker) MEWPS, a rescue plan must also be produced to recover an operative who has fallen from the basket, this could be a simple as lowering the boom if this is possible from ground level.
- Do not climb out of a MEWP or attempt to over reach from the cage.
- At the end of the working day plant must be refuelled and left secure (forks flat on the ground, hand brake on and plant securely locked and immobilised). Keys must be handed in to the approved point.

Each category requires a separate operator's certificate.

Only nationally approved certificates *issued* by one of the following organisations should be accepted:

- Construction Skills (formally Construction Industry Training Board – CITB)
- Construction Plant Certification Scheme

- The Independent Training Standards Scheme and Register (ITSSAR) (the administrative arm of the Association of Industrial Truck Trainers)
- National Plant Operators Registration Scheme
- RTITB (formally Road Traffic Industry Training Board)
- International Powered Access Federation (IPAF)

Caution fork-lift trucks operating

No fork lift trucks beyond this point

Lifting Appliances, Equipment and Rigging

- All lifting operations (rigging work) must be planed and supervised by a competent person in accordance with the Lifting Operations Lifting Equipment Regulations 1998. These regulations are an addition to Provision and Use of Work Equipment Regulations 1998 and should be read in conjunction.

- Lifting appliances will only be operated by competent and authorised personnel. Riggers are very skilled operatives; they are in fact lifting engineers and should not be seen as truss monkeys who simply work at height.

- Appropriate evidence of thorough examinations and or testing having been carried out in respect of all Lifting Appliances and Lifting Equipment must be available for inspection before use. Test/inspection certificates should travel with the equipment.

- Lifting equipment includes: truss, rigging motors, steels, truss, round slings, "O" and "D" rings, shackles, etc. The regulations also cover cranes and tail lifts on trucks, MEWPS and lift trucks.

- Structures and ground surfaces from which Lifting Appliances will operate will be adequately constructed and prepared to ensure as far as practicable the stability of the appliance during use and monitored accordingly.

- Practical steps will be taken to prevent falling and spillages of materials.

- Where necessary barriers and fencing will be erected to protect operatives and other persons who may be affected by the rigging and lifting operations.

- Safe working loads and working load limits of appliances or equipment must not be exceeded.

- A competent person must be responsible to carry out inspections. Thorough examinations and compilation of records as necessary.

- The venue or staging company must be provided with the "rigging plot" well in advance so it can be assessed to ensure the venue or stage structure can support the proposed loadings.

- Sites must be checked for proximity hazards before use of any Lifting Appliances and necessary precautions taken in respect of signs, barriers, etc.

- Risk Assessments must be prepared for all Rigging Operations.

- Where necessary a Method Statement will be prepared before any lifting operations are commenced.

- Where required, all points of rigging must have a secondary back up. Safety chains must be used on lamps and wherever else required.

- The Lifting Operations and Lifting Equipment Regulations 1998 must be complied with in all respects including the production of risk assessments and method statements.

- A written completion certificate must be completed for all rigging operations.

Work at Height

Work at Height is defined as any height where a fall could lead to injury. The Work at Height Regulations requires all work at height to be:

- properly planned,

- for the correct equipment to be selected,

- for operatives to be trained, supervised and risk assessed and,

- if required, provision to rescue an operative from height in an emergency will be required and a written rescue plan produced in advance – operatives to be trained in rescue techniques and rescue equipment available on site.

Only those who are trained, fully equipped and authorised are permitted to climb and / or use access equipment. Training applies to every method of access including ladders, steps, scaffold access towers, MEWPS, rope access and fall arrest systems. Permission to work at height must first be given by the person in charge (such as the Stage

Manager) who should ensure a safe working area and hard hat zones are established before work at height commences.

A safe place of work must be established and suitable PPE must be used including climbing helmets and safety footwear for all work at height. Suitable PPE for fall arrest will generally consist of a fall arrest harness, connectors, shock absorber and fall arrest lanyards.

Areas below aerial work activities to be cleared of all personnel as appropriate. Those working below (out of necessity such as ground riggers) must not walk or stand below a climber working overhead; they must also be equipped with helmets, etc.

Stillages, flight cases and equipment must not be left under a climber in case of a fall.

A written rescue plan and rescue system must in place before starting work at height using fall arrest, rope access systems or cherry picker type MEWPS. Operatives must be trained in rescue from height.

No work at height should be carried out if environmental hazards jeopardise health and safety.

The Regulations set out a simple hierarchy for managing and selecting equipment for work at height:

Duty Holders must:

- Avoid work at height where they can.

- Use work equipment or other measures to prevent falls where they cannot avoid working at height; and

- where they cannot eliminate the risk of a fall, use work equipment or other measures to minimise the distance and consequences of a fall should one occur.

Do not borrow, loan or share fall arrest or rope access equipment.

Truck drivers, etc. must not be allowed to climb using truss ladders or use fall arrest equipment to access followspot positions. They are not trained, insured or equipped for such activities and this may infringe on the permitted working hours for a driver.

Climbers *must* inspect their own fall arrest equipment each day before use.

Avoid mud, dirt, sharp edges and chemicals (such as battery acid) that can easily damage rope or webbing and other equipment. Store your equipment out of direct sunlight that can damage ropes and webbing.

Before climbing, tie back long hair, remove any jewellery and empty your pockets.

Ensure any tools and equipment that you carry while climbing are on a lanyard so they can't fall if dropped.

During the climb, always maintain three points of contact i.e. one foot, two hands, etc.

Work at height must be avoided if possible; working from the ground is preferable.

Access systems should be chosen following this hierarchy:

1. access stairs and protected gantry or walk ways
2. access towers, scaffold or platforms, MEWP (Mobile Elevating Work Platform)
3. rope access systems
4. ladders or steps
5. climbing using fall arrest systems

Fall arrest is the "last resort" as the system is only protective and not preventative.

Ladders and Steps

- Only Class 1 Industrial Heavy Duty or Trade Ladders (BS EN131) that are free from defect must be used. Domestic ladders must not be used.

- Operatives must be properly trained; information on training can be obtained from the Ladder Association.

- All ladders will be inspected by a competent person on at least an annual basis and quick visual inspection by the user before use. "Ladder tags" should be used to identify all ladders and record inspection information.

- Ladders must be secured at the top at each stile by lashing or proper clamps. If not practicable they can be staked at the base, footed or weighed down.

- Ladders must be pitched out to a 75° angle and must rise as least five rungs above a place of landing or secured alongside an upright handhold.

- Ladders and steps should be free from obstruction at the base area and should be pitched plumb, either with a levelling device or prepared base.

- Only one person at a time should be allowed on a ladder.

- Heavy materials or tools must not be carried – either ascending or descending ladders or steps.

- Ladders should be used only for access or light work of short duration.

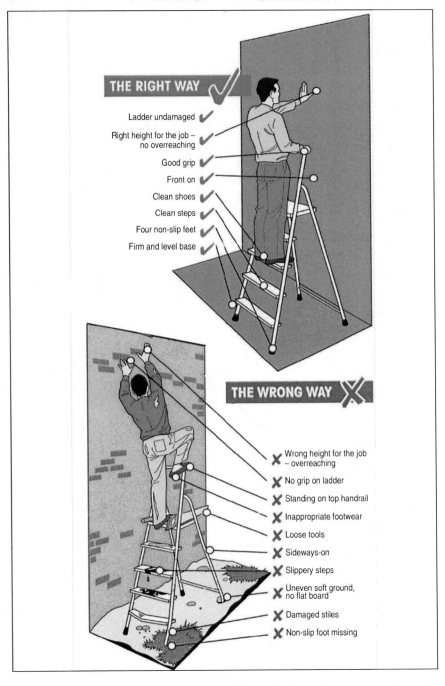

THE RIGHT WAY ✓

Ladder undamaged ✓
Right height for the job –
no overreaching ✓
Good grip ✓
Front on ✓
Clean shoes ✓
Clean steps ✓
Four non-slip feet ✓
Firm and level base ✓

THE WRONG WAY ✗

✗ Wrong height for the job
– overreaching
✗ No grip on ladder
✗ Standing on top handrail
✗ Inappropriate footwear
✗ Loose tools
✗ Sideways-on
✗ Slippery steps
✗ Uneven soft ground,
no flat board
✗ Damaged stiles
✗ Non-slip foot missing

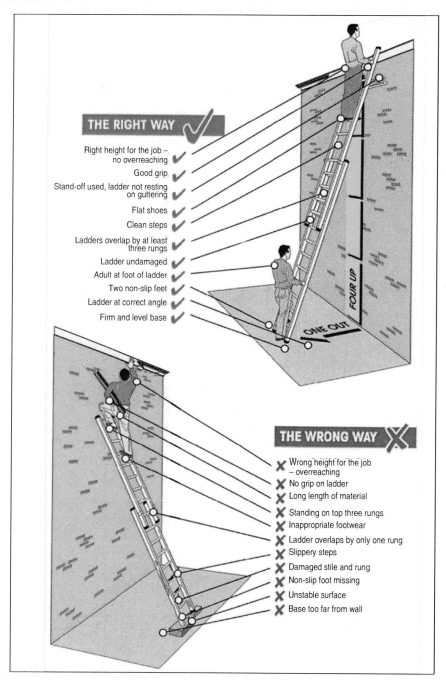

THE RIGHT WAY ✓

Right height for the job – no overreaching

Good grip

Stand-off used, ladder not resting on guttering

Flat shoes

Clean steps

Ladders overlap by at least three rungs

Ladder undamaged

Adult at foot of ladder

Two non-slip feet

Ladder at correct angle

Firm and level base

FOUR UP

ONE OUT

THE WRONG WAY ✗

✗ Wrong height for the job – overreaching

✗ No grip on ladder

✗ Long length of material

✗ Standing on top three rungs

✗ Inappropriate footwear

✗ Ladder overlaps by only one rung

✗ Slippery steps

✗ Damaged stile and rung

✗ Non-slip foot missing

✗ Unstable surface

✗ Base too far from wall

Access Towers

- Mobile access towers or scaffolds should be erected to BS 5973 standards; the Prefabricated Aluminium Structures Manufactures Association (PASMA) Code of Practice and manufactures instructions.

- Before use a competent person (holder of a PASMA certificate) will inspect mobile towers or scaffolding and sign it off.

- Bay width and loading tables will be strictly adhered to.

- Guardrails and (if fitted) toe boards will be maintained in good order.

- All components will be inspected to ensure good condition.

- Sole boards, not less than 1,000 square cm, will be fitted under base plates, other than on concrete or steel surfaces.

- Mobile towers will not be moved from the base.

- Stabilisers will be fitted and used on all mobile towers.

- No person is permitted to remain on a tower during the moving or repositioning of the tower.

- Work platforms and scaffolds should not be overloaded and materials stacked to prevent falling.

- All persons in charge of erecting aluminium access towers must hold current PASMA (Prefabricated Access Suppliers' and Manufacturers' Association) Certificate.

Work restraint, Rope Access and Fall Arrest Systems

Definitions:

Work restraint systems and equipment will include a lanyard which must be adjusted, or set, to a fixed length to prevent the user physically getting to a place where they could fall, e.g. a platform edge or fragile surface.

Rope access systems use two ropes, a working rope and a safety rope, each secured to a reliable anchor. The user's harness is attached to both ropes in such a way they can get to and from the work area and the risk of falling is prevented or limited. Rope access operatives must be trained to the standards set by the Industrial Rope Access Trade Association (IRATA).

Fall arrest systems and equipment limit the impact force of a fall on the user and prevent them hitting the ground. The anchor point should be as high as possible above the feet of the user to limit the distance of the fall. Equipment must be regularly inspected for wear and damage.

A full body harness, twin lanyard, shock absorber and connectors for fall arrest

You should only consider the use of personal fall protection equipment (fall arrest) to prevent or minimise the consequences of a fall when collective preventive measures, e.g. scaffolds and cherry pickers, are not practical. Personal fall protection equipment that prevents a fall, e.g. a work restraint system, should always take priority over personal equipment which only limits the height and/or consequences of a fall, e.g. a fall arrest system. You will need special training to use fall arrest systems safely and prove you are competent.

You should select equipment that:

- is suitable for the particular circumstances of the task, e.g. a restraint system should not be used for fall arrest.

- can be used for the particular task within its design limits, e.g. there is an adequate clearance distance.

When using fall arrest equipment:

- it must meet the standard relevant to its intended use, e.g. BS EN 361 for a full body harness;

- has compatible components so the safe function of any one component is not adversely affected by, and does not interfere with, that of another, e.g. do not use an energy-absorbing lanyard to extend an inertia reel, as this will affect the inertia reel's performance.

You will need to undertake checks and inspections:

- new equipment should be checked to make sure it is appropriate for the intended use, that it operates correctly and that it is in good condition;

- all equipment should be checked before each use;

- in addition to pre-use checks, equipment should have a detailed inspection by a competent person in accordance with a schedule drawn up by them;
- interim inspections should be made between the inspections by the competent person where a hazard that could cause significant deterioration in the equipment is present, e.g. use in acidic or alkaline environments etc;
- damaged equipment must be taken out of service immediately. Even a small cut in webbing can seriously affect performance.

You will also need to make sure:
anchors and anchor points are of adequate strength;

- where possible, anchors and anchor points are above the user so that the anchor line or lanyard is taut or has as little slack as possible; and
- there is a rescue plan in place and suitable people and equipment available to put it into effect.

The user's life depends on their personal fall protection systems and equipment being maintained properly.

Never share, loan or borrow fall arrest equipment

Equipment should be:

- kept clean and dry and properly stored.
- thoroughly dried before storage, if it has become wet.
- only altered or repaired when approved by the manufacturer.

Noise

PA systems are not the only source of noise you will come across at work; power tools, plant (it can be over 100dB (A) inside the cab of a rough terrain fork lift truck), vehicles, etc. All produce high volumes that can permanently damage your hearing.

Wherever possible, keep away from noisy environments with high sound pressure levels; rotate your work if possible.

If this is not possible use ear protection. This must be used following the manufacturer's instructions and any information and training you may have been given.

Disposable Ear Plug fitting instructions

Before fitting any ear plugs, make sure your hands are clean.

Hold the ear plug between your thumb and forefinger. Roll and compress the entire ear plug to a small, crease-free cylinder.

While still rolling, use your other hand to reach over your head and pull up and back on your outer ear. This straightens the ear canal, making way for a snug fit. Insert the ear plug and hold for 20 to 30 seconds. This allows the ear plug to expand and fill your ear canal.

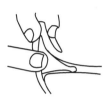

Test the fit. In a noisy environment, and with earplugs inserted, cup both hands over your ears and release. You should not notice a significant difference in the noise level. If the noise seems to lessen when your hands are cupped over your ears, your ear plugs are probably not fitted properly. Remove and refit following instructions.

Always remove ear plugs slowly, twisting them to break the seal. If you remove them too quickly, you could damage your ear drum. Use plugs once only.

Ear defenders or muffs

If damaged or not fitted/ worn correctly they should not be relied upon to protect hearing to the level required. Ensure a snug fit and seal with no hair that will break the seal of

ear muffs. Generally speaking, ear plugs provide better protection than ear muffs.

Control of Substances Hazardous to Health

No employee should use chemicals without the knowledge required to work with those chemicals safely.

Under the Control of Substances Hazardous to Health Regulations, employers have a duty to carry out risk assessments for the substances used in their workplace.

To do this they will need to look at how the substance is being used and consult the Manufacturer's Safety Data Sheet for the particular substance as well as reading the label on the container the substance was supplied in. Manufacturers have a duty to provide Safety Date Sheets.

Employees should be given a copy of the risk assessment so they know what controls they should be putting in place before using a substance. Substances can include oil, diesel, smoke fluids, paint and cleaning substances. A few simple rules apply.

Two hazardous substances have regulations all to themselves: asbestos and lead. Asbestos is still found in many buildings and should be avoided at all costs; do not attempt to handle, cut, drill, sand or remove asbestos if found. Leave it to the specialists. You should be warned if asbestos is present but don't depend on this.

Lead was used in solder and has largely been replaced but you may come across some solder containing lead. Make sure you do not inhale the fumes and use it in a well ventilated place.

Controls

- Do not mix substances.

- Store in original labelled containers – away from children and food stuffs – in a cool dry ventilated and locked cabinet.
- Do not swallow or inhale and avoid contact with skin or eyes.
- Do not dispose of substances, containers or aerosols into fires.
- Do not pour substances into drains or water courses.
- Avoid contact with heat, naked flame or sources of ignition.
- In case of contact with skin or eyes flush with copious amounts of water, remove contaminated clothing, rinse mouth with water – do not allow patient to drink – do not induce vomiting.
- Use in a well ventilated area.
- Clean up spillages immediately.
- Use PPE – rubber or latex gloves, overalls and eye protection.
- Only transport the minimum amount you really need of any substance.
- Always follow manufacturer's instructions.
- Wash your hands after using any substances.
- Do not eat, drink or smoke when handling substances.

The orange hazardous substance signs below left are being replaced with the new signs below right.

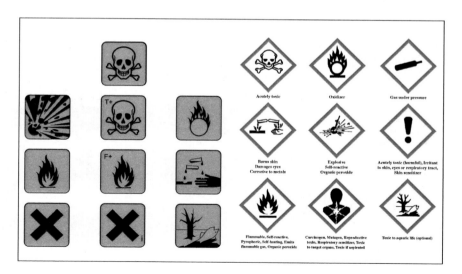

Special Effects

Strobes

Strobe lighting can induce epilepsy in some extreme cases so to reduce the risk strobes must be operated in accordance with the guidance set out in the Event Safety Guide, A Guide to Health, Safety and Welfare at Music and Similar Events.

When strobe lights are used at venues, flicker rates should be kept at or below 4 flashes per second. Below this rate it is estimated that only 5% of the flicker-sensitive population will be at risk of an attack. This flicker rate only applies to the overall output of any group of lights in direct view, but where more than one strobe light is used the flashes should be synchronised.

Everyone must be informed if strobes are to be used and warning signs must be erected if necessary.

Ultraviolet light

Powerful ultraviolet light can sensitise exposed areas of the skin in very rare cases. If any member of staff experiences skin sensitisation they should remove themselves from the area of the ultraviolet light and seek medical aid.

Ultra violet lighting must be rigged at a minimum of 16ft. away from any person who may come into contact with it during use and only used when following manufacturer's instructions and with a very high standard of safety and maintenance.

Ensure that lamps are used correctly to restrict exposure to ultraviolet radiation and in particular to UVB radiation.

To remove UVB radiation, some lamps have a double skin whereas other manufacturers provide lamp housings, which have separate filters. Lamps should not be used if the outer skin is broken or if the housing filter is not in place.

LASER BEAM

Lasers

Lasers come into a special category, do not touch or tamper with laser equipment and do not look straight into the beam of the laser to avoid possible damage to eyes. Keep at a safe distance to avoid burns.

Lamps and HMI Lamp Systems

Gauntlets covering wrist arteries, and a full face visor covering neck arteries should be worn while handing the lamps. Xenon and HMI lamps of 5 kW and 7kW are pressurised to about 8 bar when cold and around 30 bar when hot and so a lamp burst is possible with the resultant danger from flying glass. When the lamp is being installed, people should vacate the vicinity until the projector housing is closed. It is not advisable to carry out this operation with the audience present.

The arc of xenon and HMI lamps are very bright and housings are designed so that the arc cannot be viewed directly by the operator.

Care should be taken that people are not put at risk by 'blinding' them with the light, especially if they are moving around in otherwise dark environments (e.g. while entering or leaving a venue).

Smoke, Vapour and Fog Effects

Employees must follow the same basic safety rules that apply to all types of smoke machine:

- The machine must be in a fixed position and adequately protected from interference; some machines can get very hot during use.
- A competent operator should be with the machine.
- All machines must be used in accordance with the manufacturer's instructions.
- Fans may be used to direct the smoke or vapour but care must be taken to prevent the spread of smoke or vapour into public areas; this may cause an audience to panic.
- Smoke and vapour must not be discharged or allowed to drift into exits, stairways, escape routes, or be allowed to obscure exit signs or fire protection equipment. Some fluids, cracked oil in particular, leave a deposit on stage which can prove a dangerous slip hazard.

If fire or smoke detection equipment is fitted within a venue special care must be taken. Some venues and Entertainment Licence conditions do not allow the use of smoke or fog machines because of these detectors.

If they are in use the amount of smoke or fog must be restricted to prevent these detectors operating. On no account must employees try to prevent smoke detectors operating by covering them, overriding or switching them off.

Some smoke fluids are known to cause discomfort to those who suffer from smoke allergy or asthma. Avoid the use of such fluids where possible.

Weather

Bad weather can make conditions on site and on roads very dangerous – rain, wind and mud being the three worst factors.

The temptation to rush jobs or skimp on safety matters must be resisted and even more care must be taken with electrical safety. Vehicles and equipment may get stuck in mud and need to be towed out. If this is the case, stewards must be used to keep onlookers at a safe distance and only chains or tow ropes used that are well within the safe working loads. The use of temporary roadway should be considered. Forklift trucks must never be used for towing other vehicles.

Extra care must be taken with vehicles, plant and machinery to prevent slipping and skidding in wet and muddy conditions. Staff must attend for work with suitable warm and waterproof clothing and footwear in cold and/or wet weather and suitable sun block (Factor 15 or above) and covering for the skin to prevent burning or sun stroke in hot sunny weather.

Long term exposure to the sun will speed up ageing of the skin and increases the chance of skin cancer in later life. Staff are advised to keep there tops on and wear a wide brimmed hat to protect the head, face and neck from the sun's harmful ultraviolet rays. In hot weather staff should drink plenty of liquid but not alcohol. Try to avoid working in the sun, and rotate work operations to avoid the sun. Working in the sun can be very stressful and judgement can be impaired with the onset of even minor heat exhaustion. Seek prompt medical advice if you think you have a skin problem.

Dehydration can be a very dangerous condition and often the victim does not even feel thirsty. Symptoms are dizziness, dry mouth, no or low urine output and generally feeling ill. Severe cases can be life threatening so drink plenty of water when doing hard physical work or when working in a hot climate.

Greenfield Sites

Green field sites contain a number of additional hazards not encountered elsewhere; these include Lime Disease, Ring Worm, Tetanus and Leptospirosis (also known as Weils Disease).

Where ever possible employees should keep away from hedges and fences to avoid cuts, scratches, thorns, brambles and barbed wire.

The soil on outdoor sites is likely to be contaminated by animals with Tetanus.

Any person who suffers a wound from one these sources should seek medical assistance and advice as these wounds can be contaminated by Tetanus.

Employees should cover all broken skin with waterproof plasters before starting work and wear P.P.E. such as gloves. Wash your hands after work and always before eating, drinking or smoking.

Employees are advised to keep up to date with anti-tetanus vaccinations from their GP and to have all cuts obtained on outdoor sites examined by a doctor.

Employees must not climb trees, walls or other objects and structures on outdoor sites unless the structure has been specifically installed and designed to be climbed and all safety precautions and procedures are strictly followed.

Wherever possible employees should stay clear of ponds, lakes, streams, rivers, ditches, pools and puddles and never wash hands in such bodies of water as they may contain a bacteria infection known as Leptospirosis. This disease is carried by rats and cattle in their urine.

This is a serious and sometimes fatal infection that can enter the body through small cuts and scratches and through the lining of the mouth throat and eyes after contact with infected water and urine. It may also contaminate cattle feed stuffs on farms. All sightings of rats should be reported.

Employees should cover all broken skin with waterproof plasters before starting work and wear P.P.E. such as gloves, Wellington boots and barrier cream. This is especially important when collecting in equipment (particularly cables) after a show that may have become contaminated with sewage, vomit or urine (human or animal). Wash your hands after work (with soap, water and antiseptic) and always before eating, drinking or smoking. Try to avoid involuntarily actions such as rubbing the face, nose, mouth or eyes.

If any employee suspects they may have been in contact with Leptospirosis, especially if they develop a flu-like illness and severe headache they should report to a doctor as soon as possible and state that you suspect you may have contacted Leptospirosis. If treated promptly, Leptospirosis is much less severe.

Display Screen Equipment (DSE)

We seem to be using more a more computers and display screen equipment in our work and once again employers have a duty to risk assess display screen equipment and work stations.

The Regulations apply where staff habitually use VDUs as a significant part of their normal work.

Other people, who use VDUs only occasionally, are not covered by the requirements in the Regulations (apart from the workstation requirements). However, their employers still have general duties to protect them under other health and safety at work legislation.

The Regulations do not place any duties on the self-employed. However, parts of them apply if you habitually use a VDU for a significant part of your normal work and are using a client employer's workstation. The client employer has to assess and reduce risks, ensure the workstation complies with the minimum requirements and provide information, as if you were an employee. But there is no requirement for employers to plan work breaks, or provide eye tests or training for the self-employed.

Some users may get aches and pains in their hands, wrists, arms, neck, shoulders or back, especially after long periods of uninterrupted VDU work. 'Repetitive strain injury' (RSI) has become a popular term for these aches, pains and disorders, but can be misleading – it means different things to different people. A better medical name for this whole group of conditions is 'upper limb disorders'. Usually these disorders do not last, but in a few cases they may become persistent or even disabling.

Extensive research has found no evidence that VDUs can cause disease or permanent damage to eyes. But long spells of VDU work can lead to tired eyes and discomfort. Also, by giving your eyes more demanding tasks, it might make you aware of an eyesight problem you had not noticed before. You and your employer can help your eyes by ensuring your VDU is well positioned and properly adjusted, and that the workplace lighting is suitable. Ask for an eye test if you still think there is a problem. Your employer also has a duty to pay for a basic pair of glasses if required.

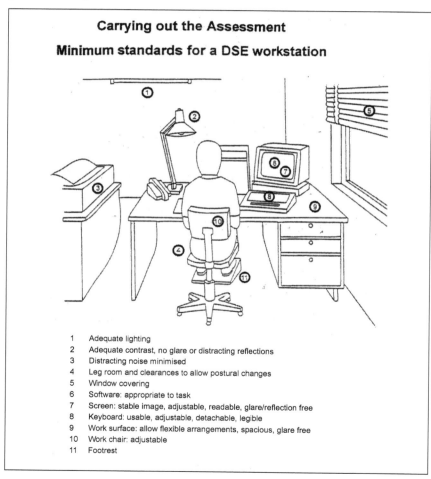

Carrying out the Assessment

Minimum standards for a DSE workstation

1   Adequate lighting
2   Adequate contrast, no glare or distracting reflections
3   Distracting noise minimised
4   Leg room and clearances to allow postural changes
5   Window covering
6   Software: appropriate to task
7   Screen: stable image, adjustable, readable, glare/reflection free
8   Keyboard: usable, adjustable, detachable, legible
9   Work surface: allow flexible arrangements, spacious, glare free
10   Work chair: adjustable
11   Footrest

Emergency Evacuation Procedures

In the event of the fire alarm being activated, or in any other emergency situation (such as a bomb scare or gas leak), all employees must leave the building or venue by the nearest available exit and assemble at the designated assembly point.

Upon arrival at a new or unfamiliar work place staff should make themselves familiar with the position of all emergency exit doors/routes, fire fighting equipment such as extinguishers, fire blankets, the means of raising the alarm and the designated assemble point.

1. If you discover a fire, however small, raise the alarm by using the break glass points, by phone, radio, shouting or whatever system exists where you are working, then call the fire brigade by:

   – **Telephone – Dial 999 or 112**

   – Give the operator your telephone number and ask for the fire brigade.

   – When the brigade replies give the call distinctly:

   – **"FIRE AT (GIVE NAME AND ADDRESS OF VENUE OR PREMISES)**

2. The premises should be evacuated by stewards or members of staff. Act calmly and leave the building or venue by using the nearest available exit. Do not wait to collect personal belongings and do not use lifts. If it is safe to do so, close windows and doors and turn off equipment, gas and electricity. Go to the Fire Assembly Point if there is one designated, if not remain outside at a safe distance.

3. **NO ONE SHOULD RE-ENTER THE PREMISES UNTIL TOLD BY A FIRE BRIGADE OFFICER THAT IT IS SAFE TO DO SO.**

Tackling a Fire

Your first priority is to raise the alarm before attempting to tackle a fire. Only tackle a fire if it is safe to do so. Ensure that you always have a clear escape route; if you can't put the fire out with one extinguisher then do not make a further attempt with another extinguisher – leave it to the professionals.

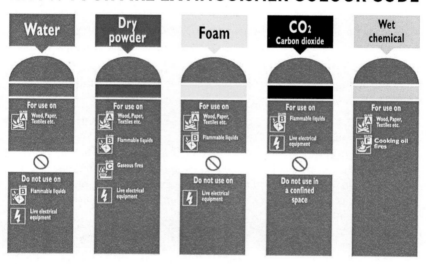

KNOW YOUR FIRE EXTINGUISHER COLOUR CODE

Make sure you know the correct extinguisher to use!

	A — Fires involving freely burning materials e.g. wood, paper, textiles & other carbonaceous materials	B — Fires involving flammable liquids e.g. petrols and spirits NOT ALCOHOL OR COOKING OIL	C — Fires involving flammable gases e.g. butane and propane	⚡ — Fires involving electrical equipment e.g. photocopiers, fax machines and computers	D (METAL) — Fires involving flammable metals e.g. magnesium and lithium	F — Fires involving cooking oil and fat e.g. olive oil, maize oil, lard and butter
Water	✓					
Foam	✓	✓				
ABC Dry Powder	✓	✓	✓	✓		
Dry Special Powder					✓	
CO₂ Gas		✓		✓		
Wet Chemical	✓					

First Aid, Accidents and Accident Reporting

The First Aid at Work Regulations require employers to carry out an assessment of first aid needs and then make adequate first aid provision for their employees even when they are out on site and away from base, they can't expect the promoter or venue to provide first aid cover for you.

A self-employed person should carry a simple first aid kit that is suitable to treat themselves at work.

Ensure you know the location of first aiders and first aid equipment where you are working and learn first aid.

All accidents and "near hits" no matter how trivial must be reported in your employers Accident Book. You may also be required to fill in the venue, promoters or production company accident book.

If you are making a report but did not see the incident only state what you actually saw. For instance, if a work-mate falls off a chair when changing a light bulb but you did not see him or her fall you will report as follows: "Fred said he fell off a chair when changing a light bulb".

Major Injuries

If there is an accident connected with work and a member of staff or self-employed person working sustains a major injury, or a member of the public suffers an injury and is taken to hospital from the site of the accident, you must notify your employer who will in turn notify the Authorities by the quickest possible means (usually by phone) and then (within 15 days) make a report under the Reporting of Incidents, Diseases and Dangerous Occurrence Regulations 2013..

All accidents must be immediately notified to your employer. You may also be required to fill in the Promoters, Production Companies or Venues Accident Book if asked as well as your employers Accident Book.

Reportable Major Injuries are:

- Fracture, other than to fingers, thumbs and toes;
- Amputation;
- Dislocation of the shoulder, hip, knee or spine;
- Loss of sight (temporary or permanent);
- Chemical or hot metal burn to the eye or any penetrating injury to the eye;
- Injury resulting from an electric shock or electrical burn leading to unconsciousness, or requiring resuscitation or admittance to hospital for more than 24 hours;
- Any other injury: leading to hypothermia, heat-induced illness or unconsciousness; or requiring resuscitation; or requiring admittance to hospital for more than 24 hours;
- Unconsciousness caused by asphyxia or exposure to harmful substance or biological agent;

- Acute illness requiring medical treatment, or loss of consciousness arising from absorption of any substance by inhalation, ingestion or through the skin;
- Acute illness requiring medical treatment where there is reason to believe that this resulted from exposure to a biological agent or its toxins or infected material.

Reportable Over Seven Day Injuries

If there is an accident connected with work (including an act of physical violence) and an employee, or a self-employed person suffers an over-seven-day injury then it must be reported by the employer and to the enforcing authority within fifteen days. An over-seven-day injury is one which is not "major" but results in the injured person being away from work OR unable to do the full range of their normal duties for more than seven days.

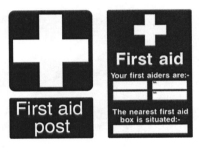

Environmental Safety and Protection

Probably the mains areas of pollution we are likely to come across are from noise, waste, exhaust fumes and oil spillage.

Environmental management systems should be in place to:

- Minimise waste
- Control noise so that it does not cause a nuisance to neighbors
- Use energy efficiently

Employers have a duty to instruct, inform and train staff in:

- Legal requirements of pollution control
- Cause and prevention of pollution

- Reporting procedures
- Emergency response
- Waste minimisation and segregation
- Safe storage and disposal of waste materials

Employees and self-employed person's duties:

- Do not dispose of waste except in approved way
- Do NOT pour oil/chemicals down drains or into water courses
- only dispose of chemicals in an approved way
- Segregate waste and place it in the correct bin or skip
- Never burn rubbish
- Learn were the spill kit is and how to use it
- Keep your waste to a minimum
- Only store waste in a safe area
- Diesel must only be stored and transported in bunded tanks and bowsers.

A bunded fuel bowser

Safety Culture

We hope this has given you enough information to help you to contribute to a positive safety culture for this industry. There is no single definition of "a safety culture". It is a term best used to describe the way in which safety is managed in the workplace, and often reflects "the attitudes, beliefs, perceptions and values that employees share in relation to safety".

A safety culture is one in which safety is regarded by everyone as being an issue which concerns everyone. As a result, safety rules are understood and adhered to and negative and macho attitudes to safety ('we could not work if we followed health and safety regulations'/'hard hats are for wimps') go out of the window.

Plant Operator's Daily Check List	
to be completed once every day	
Operator's name...Date.......................	
Machine type...	
Horn	*working and clearly audible*
Lock	*machine must be lockable with a removable key to keep it secure from unintentional use*
Brakes	*in safe working order*
Steering system	*in safe working order*
Tyres	*correctly fitted, in good condition and (if pneumatic) correctly inflated. Correct tyre pressures should be clearly marked on the machine. Pneumatic tyres on rough terrain machines must be fitted with dust caps.*
Lights (if fitted)	*in good working order.*
Warning beacon	*in good working order.*
All controls	*should be clearly marked so that they can be seen from the operator's position.*
Safe load indicator (if fitted)	*must be in good working order.*
Oil, water, battery, fuel	*Check for leaks and that all fluids are to correct level.*
Hydraulics	*Visual check on hoses and connections for wear and leaks*
Overall visual check on the general condition of the machine or plant.	
Operators hand book	Must be provided by hire company and be present with the machine.

Plant Operator's Daily Check List	
to be completed once every day	
Certificate of last test/ examination	Required under Lifting Operations, Lifting Equipment Regulations, must be provided by hire company and be present with the machine.

I..(operators name)
have examined the above machine and found it suitable/unsuitable for use.

I have found the faults indicated and have reported these faults to
....
(name of person to whom faults have been reported).

Signed... (Operator)

Signed...
(Person to whom faults have been reported)

**THE MACHINE MUST NOT BE USED UNTIL
ALL FAULTS HAVE BEEN RECTIFIED**

Health and Safety Management in the Live Music and Events Industry

by Chris Hannam

Now available from Entertainment Technology Press Ltd

The Studio, High Green, Great Shelford, Cambridge, CB22 5EG UK

www.etbooks.co.uk

First published in October 2004, Chris Hannam's major work on Health and Safety Management in the live music and events sector has been substantially revised. The title covers applications regarding all aspects of staging live entertainment events, and is an invaluable manual for managers and event organisers.

The book includes well thought-out and easy to understand sections on Risk Assessment and Safety Method Statements, Effective Health and Safety Policy, Selection of Personnel, Crowd Management, Communications, Performance Management, Environmental Safety to name but a few, as well as comprehensive chapters on all of the legal frameworks for Machinery, Fire Safety, Work Equipment, Employers Liability, Occupiers Liability, Accident Reporting and RIDDOR, PPE, Working at Height, LOLER, Special Effects, Temporary Structures, First Aid, Traffic Management, COSHH, Working Time Regulations and many more, this text covers all of the HSE and non-HSE publications in a well-managed and logical handbook.

Reviewing the second edition for Entertainment Technology magazine, John-Paul Greenock says: "Chris Hannam's book is an essential text for anyone who works within the Live Production Industry and should be the standard guide for promotion via our trade bodies. It dovetails effortlessly with the Event Safety Guide (Purple Guide) and sits effectively alongside the long awaited Safety Passport Scheme run under the Production Services Association. Chris, a leading provider of the scheme in the UK, initially introduced the idea of Safety Passports to the PSA, and subsequently developed the course as part of a safety passport working group. "I am pleased to have re-discovered, and thoroughly recommend Health and Safety Management in the Live Music and Events Industry, by one of the world's leading industry experts."

ENTERTAINMENT TECHNOLOGY PRESS

FREE SUBSCRIPTION SERVICE

Keeping Up To Date with

Health and Safety in the Live Music and Event Technical Production Industry

Entertainment Technology titles are continually up-dated, and all major changes and additions are listed in date order in the relevant dedicated area of the publisher's website. Simply go to the front page of www.etnow.com and click on the BOOKS button. From there you can locate the title and be connected through to the latest information and services related to the publication.

The author of the title welcomes comments and suggestions about the book and can be contacted by email at: info@stagesafe.co.uk

Titles Published by Entertainment Technology Press

50 Rigging Calls *Chris Higgs, Cristiano Giavedoni 246pp* **£16.95**
ISBN: 9781904031758
Chris Higgs, author of ETP's two leading titles on rigging, An Introduction to Rigging in the Entertainment Industry and Rigging for Entertainment: Regulations and Practice, has collected together 50 articles he has provided regularly for Lighting + Sound International magazine from 2005 to date. They provide a wealth of information for those practising the craft within the entertainment technology industry. The book is profusely illustrated with caricature drawings by Christiano Giavedoni, featuring the popular rigging expert Mario.

ABC of Theatre Jargon *Francis Reid 106pp* **£9.95** ISBN: 9781904031093
This glossary of theatrical terminology explains the common words and phrases that are used in normal conversation between actors, directors, designers, technicians and managers.

Aluminium Structures in the Entertainment Industry *Peter Hind 234pp* **£24.95**
ISBN: 9781904031062
Aluminium Structures in the Entertainment Industry aims to educate the reader in all aspects of the design and safe usage of temporary and permanent aluminium structures specific to the entertainment industry – such as roof structures, PA towers, temporary staging, etc.

Autocad – A Handbook for Theatre Users *David Ripley 340pp* **£29.95**
ISBN: 9781904031741
From 'Setting Up' to 'Drawing in Three Dimensions' via 'Drawings Within Drawings', this compact and fully illustrated guide to AutoCAD covers everything from the basics to full colour rendering and remote 3D plotting. Third, completely revised edition, June 2014.

Automation in the Entertainment Industry – A User's Guide *Mark Ager and John Hastie 382pp* **£29.95** ISBN: 9781904031581
In the last 15 years, there has been a massive growth in the use of automation in entertainment, especially in theatres, and it is now recognised as its own discipline. However, it is still only used in around 5% of theatres worldwide. In the next 25 years, given current growth patterns, that figure will rise to 30%. This will mean that the majority of theatre personnel, including directors, designers, technical staff, actors and theatre management, will come into contact with automation for the first time at some point in their careers. This book is intended to provide insights and practical advice from those who use automation, to help the first-time user understand the issues and avoid the pitfalls in its implementation.

Basics – A Beginner's Guide to Lighting Design *Peter Coleman 92pp* **£9.95**
ISBN: 9781904031413
The fourth in the author's 'Basics' series, this title covers the subject area in four main sections: The Concept, Practical Matters, Related Issues and The Design Into Practice. In an

area that is difficult to be definitive, there are several things that cross all the boundaries of all lighting design and it's these areas that the author seeks to help with.

Basics – A Beginner's Guide to Special Effects *Peter Coleman 82pp* **£9.95**
ISBN: 9781904031338
This title introduces newcomers to the world of special effects. It describes all types of special effects including pyrotechnic, smoke and lighting effects, projections, noise machines, etc. It places emphasis on the safe storage, handling and use of pyrotechnics.

Basics – A Beginner's Guide to Stage Lighting *Peter Coleman 86pp* **£9.95**
ISBN: 9781904031208
This title does what it says: it introduces newcomers to the world of stage lighting. It will not teach the reader the art of lighting design, but will teach beginners much about the 'nuts and bolts' of stage lighting.

Basics – A Beginner's Guide to Stage Sound *Peter Coleman 86pp* **£9.95**
ISBN: 9781904031277
This title does what it says: it introduces newcomers to the world of stage sound. It will not teach the reader the art of sound design, but will teach beginners much about the background to sound reproduction in a theatrical environment.

Basics: A Beginner's Guide to Stage Management *Peter Coleman 64pp* **£7.95**
ISBN: 9781904031475
The fifth in Peter Coleman's popular 'Basics' series, this title provides a practical insight into, and the definition of, the role of stage management. Further chapters describe Cueing or 'Calling' the Show (the Prompt Book), and the Hardware and Training for Stage Management. This is a book about people and systems, without which most of the technical equipment used by others in the performance workplace couldn't function.

Building Better Theaters *Michael Mell 180pp* **£16.95** ISBN: 9781904031406
A title within our Consultancy Series, this book describes the process of designing a theatre, from the initial decision to build through to opening night. Michael Mell's book provides a step-by-step guide to the design and construction of performing arts facilities. Chapters discuss: assembling your team, selecting an architect, different construction methods, the architectural design process, construction of the theatre, theatrical systems and equipment, the stage, backstage, the auditorium, ADA requirements and the lobby. Each chapter clearly describes what to expect and how to avoid surprises. It is a must-read for architects, planners, performing arts groups, educators and anyone who may be considering building or renovating a theatre.

Carry on Fading *Francis Reid 216pp* **£20.00** ISBN: 9781904031642
This is a record of five of the best years of the author's life. Years so good that the only downside is the pangs of guilt at enjoying such contentment in a world full of misery induced by greed, envy and imposed ideologies. Fortunately Francis' DNA is high on luck, optimism and blessing counting.

Case Studies in Crowd Management
Chris Kemp, Iain Hill, Mick Upton, Mark Hamilton 206pp **£16.95**
ISBN: 9781904031482
This important work has been compiled from a series of research projects carried out by the staff of the Centre for Crowd Management and Security Studies at Buckinghamshire Chilterns University College (now Bucks New University), and seminar work carried out in Berlin and Groningen with partner Yourope. It includes case studies, reports and a crowd management safety plan for a major outdoor rock concert, safe management of rock concerts utilising a triple barrier safety system and pan-European Health & Safety Issues.

Case Studies in Crowd Management, Security and Business Continuity
Chris Kemp, Patrick Smith 274pp **£24.95** ISBN: 9781904031635
The creation of good case studies to support work in progress and to give answers to those seeking guidance in their quest to come to terms with perennial questions is no easy task. The first Case Studies in Crowd Management book focused mainly on a series of festivals and events that had a number of issues which required solving. This book focuses on a series of events that had major issues that impacted on the every day delivery of the events researched.

Close Protection – The Softer Skills *Geoffrey Padgham 132pp* **£11.95**
ISBN: 9781904031390
This is the first educational book in a new 'Security Series' for Entertainment Technology Press, and it coincides with the launch of the new 'Protective Security Management' Foundation Degree at Buckinghamshire Chilterns University College (now Bucks New University). The author is a former full-career Metropolitan Police Inspector from New Scotland Yard with 27 years' experience of close protection (CP). For 22 of those years he specialised in operations and senior management duties with the Royalty Protection Department at Buckingham Palace, followed by five years in the private security industry specialising in CP training design and delivery. His wealth of protection experience comes across throughout the text, which incorporates sound advice and exceptional practical guidance, subtly separating fact from fiction. This publication is an excellent form of reference material for experienced operatives, students and trainees.

A Comparative Study of Crowd Behaviour at Two Major Music Events
Chris Kemp, Iain Hill, Mick Upton 78pp **£7.95** ISBN: 9781904031253
A compilation of the findings of reports made at two major live music concerts, and in particular crowd behaviour, which is followed from ingress to egress.

Control Freak *Wayne Howell 270pp* **£28.95** ISBN: 9781904031550
Control Freak is the second book by Wayne Howell. It provides an in depth study of DMX512 and the new RDM (Remote Device Management) standards. The book is aimed at both users and developers and provides a wealth of real world information based on the author's twenty year experience of lighting control.

Copenhagen Opera House *Richard Brett and John Offord 272pp* **£32.00**
ISBN: 9781904031420
Completed in a little over three years, the Copenhagen Opera House opened with a royal gala performance on 15th January 2005. Built on a spacious brown-field site, the building is a landmark venue and this book provides the complete technical background story to an opera house set to become a benchmark for future design and planning. Sixteen chapters by relevant experts involved with the project cover everything from the planning of the auditorium and studio stage, the stage engineering, stage lighting and control and architectural lighting through to acoustic design and sound technology plus technical summaries.

Cue 80 *Francis Reid 310pp* **£17.95** ISBN: 9781904031659
Although Francis Reid's work in theatre has been visual rather than verbal, writing has provided crucial support. Putting words on paper has been the way in which he organised and clarified his thoughts. And in his self-confessed absence of drawing skills, writing has helped him find words to communicate his visual thinking in discussions with the rest of the creative team. As a by-product, this process of searching for the right words to help formulate and analyse ideas has resulted in half-a-century of articles in theatre journals. Cue 80 is an anthology of these articles and is released in celebration of Francis' 80th birthday.

The DMX 512-A Handbook – Design and Implementation of DMX Enabled Products and Networks *James Eade 150pp* **£13.95** ISBN: 9781904031727
This guidebook was originally conceived as a guide to the new DMX512-A standard on behalf of the ESTA Controls Protocols Working Group (CPWG). It has subsequently been updated and is aimed at all levels of reader from technicians working with or servicing equipment in the field as well as manufacturers looking to build in DMX control to their lighting products. It also gives thorough guidance to consultants and designers looking to design DMX networks.

Electric Shadows: an Introduction to Video and Projection on Stage *Nick Moran 234pp* **£23.95** ISBN: 9781904031734
Electric Shadows aims to guide the emerging video designer through the many simple and difficult technical and aesthetic choices and decisions he or she has to make in taking their design from outline idea through to realisation. The main body of the book takes the reader through the process of deciding what content will be projected onto what screen or screens to make the best overall production design. The book will help you make electric shadows that capture the attention of your audience, to help you tell your stories in just the way you want.

Electrical Safety for Live Events *Marco van Beek 98pp* **£16.95** ISBN: 9781904031284
This title covers electrical safety regulations and good practise pertinent to the entertainment industries and includes some basic electrical theory as well as clarifying the "do's and don't's" of working with electricity.

Entertainment in Production Volume 1: 1994-1999 *Rob Halliday 254pp* **£24.95**
ISBN: 9781904031512

Entertainment in Production Volume 2: 2000-2006 *Rob Halliday 242poo* £24.95
ISBN: 9781904031529
Rob Halliday has a dual career as a lighting designer/programmer and author and in these
two volumes he provides the intriguing but comprehensive technical background stories
behind the major musical productions and other notable projects spanning the period 1994
to 2005. Having been closely involved with the majority of the events described, the author
is able to present a first-hand and all-encompassing portrayal of how many of the major
shows across the past decade came into being. From *Oliver!* and *Miss Saigon* to *Mamma
Mia!* and *Mary Poppins*, here the complete technical story unfolds. The books, which are
profusely illustrated, are in large part an adapted selection of articles that first appeared in
the magazine *Lighting&Sound International*.

Entertainment Technology Yearbook 2008 *John Offord 220pp* **£14.95**
ISBN: 9781904031543
The Entertainment Technology Yearbook 2008 covers the year 2007 and includes picture
coverage of major industry exhibitions in Europe compiled from the pages of Entertainment
Technology magazine and the etnow.com website, plus articles and pictures of production,
equipment and project highlights of the year.

The Exeter Theatre Fire *David Anderson 202pp* **£24.95** ISBN: 9781904031130
This title is a fascinating insight into the events that led up to the disaster at the Theatre
Royal, Exeter, on the night of September 5th 1887. The book details what went wrong, and
the lessons that were learned from the event.

Fading into Retirement *Francis Reid 124pp* **£17.95**
ISBN: 9781904031352
This is the final book in Francis Reid's fading trilogy which, with Fading Light and Carry
on Fading, updates the Hearing the Light record of places visited, performances seen,
and people met. Never say never, but the author uses the 'final' label because decreasing
mobility means that his ability to travel is diminished to the point that his life is now
contained within a very few square miles. His memories are triggered by over 600 CDs, half
of them Handel and 100 or so DVDs supplemented by a rental subscription to LOVEFiLM.

Fading Light – A Year in Retirement *Francis Reid 136pp* **£14.95**
ISBN: 9781904031352
Francis Reid, the lighting industry's favourite author, describes a full year in retirement.
"Old age is much more fun than I expected," he says. Fading Light describes visits and
experiences to the author's favourite theatres and opera houses, places of relaxation and re-
visits to scholarly institutions.

Focus on Lighting Technology *Richard Cadena 120pp* **£17.95** ISBN: 9781904031147
This concise work unravels the mechanics behind modern performance lighting and appeals

to designers and technicians alike. Packed with clear, easy-to-read diagrams, the book provides excellent explanations behind the technology of performance lighting.

The Followspot Guide *Nick Mobsby 450pp* **£28.95** ISBN: 9781904031499
The first in ETP's Equipment Series, Nick Mobsby's Followspot Guide tells you everything you need to know about followspots, from their history through to maintenance and usage. Its pages include a technical specification of 193 followspots from historical to the latest versions from major manufacturers.

From Ancient Rome to Rock 'n' Roll – a Review of the UK Leisure Security Industry *Mick Upton 198pp* **£14.95** ISBN: 9781904031505
From stewarding, close protection and crowd management through to his engagement as a senior consultant Mick Upton has been ever present in the events industry. A founder of ShowSec International in 1982 he was its chairman until 2000. The author has led the way on training within the sector. He set up the ShowSec Training Centre and has acted as a consultant at the Bramshill Police College. He has been prominent in the development of courses at Buckinghamshire New University where he was awarded a Doctorate in 2005. Mick has received numerous industry awards. His book is a personal account of the development and professionalism of the sector across the past 50 years.

Gobos for Image Projection *Michael Hall and Julie Harper 176pp* **£25.95**
ISBN: 9781904031628
In this first published book dedicated totally to the gobo, the authors take the reader through from the history of projection to the development of the present day gobo. And there is broad practical advice and ample reference information to back it up. A feature of the work is the inclusion, interspersed throughout the text, of comment and personal experience in the use and application of gobos from over 25 leading lighting designers worldwide.

Health and Safety Aspects in the Live Music Industry *Chris Kemp, Iain Hill 300pp* **£30.00** ISBN: 9781904031222
This major work includes chapters on various safety aspects of live event production and is written by specialists in their particular areas of expertise.

Health and Safety Management in the Live Music and Events Industry *Chris Hannam 480pp* **£25.95** ISBN: 9781904031307
This title covers the health and safety regulations and their application regarding all aspects of staging live entertainment events, and is an invaluable manual for production managers and event organisers.

Hearing the Light – 50 Years Backstage *Francis Reid 280pp* **£24.95**
ISBN: 9781904031185
This highly enjoyable memoir delves deeply into the theatricality of the industry. The author's almost fanatical interest in opera, his formative period as lighting designer at Glyndebourne and his experiences as a theatre administrator, writer and teacher make for a broad and unique background.

An Introduction to Rigging in the Entertainment Industry *Chris Higgs 272pp* **£24.95**
ISBN: 9781904031123
This title is a practical guide to rigging techniques and practices and also thoroughly covers safety issues and discusses the implications of working within recommended guidelines and regulations. Second edition revised September 2008.

Let There be Light – Entertainment Lighting Software Pioneers in Conversation
Robert Bell 390pp **£32.00** ISBN: 9781904031246
Robert Bell interviews a distinguished group of software engineers working on entertainment lighting ideas and products.

Light and Colour Filters *Michael Hall and Eddie Ruffell 286pp* **£23.95**
ISBN: 9781904031598
Written by two acknowledged and respected experts in the field, this book is destined to become the standard reference work on the subject. The title chronicles the development and use of colour filters and also describes how colour is perceived and how filters function. Up-to-date reference tables will help the practitioner make better and more specific choices of colour.

Lighting for Roméo and Juliette *John Offord 172pp* **£26.95** ISBN: 9781904031161
John Offord describes the making of the Vienna State Opera production from the lighting designer's viewpoint – from the point where director Jürgen Flimm made his decision not to use scenery or sets and simply employ the expertise of lighting designer Patrick Woodroffe.

Lighting Systems for TV Studios *Nick Mobsby 570pp* **£45.00** ISBN: 9781904031000
Lighting Systems for TV Studios, now in its second edition, is the first book specifically written on the subject and has become the 'standard' resource work for studio planning and design covering the key elements of system design, luminaires, dimming, control, data networks and suspension systems as well as detailing the infrastructure items such as cyclorama, electrical and ventilation. TV lighting principles are explained and some history on TV broadcasting, camera technology and the equipment is provided to help set the scene! The second edition includes applications for sine wave and distributed dimming, moving lights, Ethernet and new cool lamp technology.

Lighting Techniques for Theatre-in-the-Round *Jackie Staines 188pp* **£24.95**
ISBN: 9781904031017
Lighting Techniques for Theatre-in-the-Round is a unique reference source for those working on lighting design for theatre-in-the-round for the first time. It is the first title to be published specifically on the subject and it also provides some anecdotes and ideas for more challenging shows, and attempts to blow away some of the myths surrounding lighting in this format.

Lighting the Diamond Jubilee Concert *Durham Marenghi 102pp* **£19.95**
ISBN: 9781904031673
In this highly personal landmark document the show's lighting designer Durham Marenghi

pays tribute to the team of industry experts who each played an important role in bringing the Diamond Jubilee Concert to fruition, both for television and live audiences. The book contains colour production photography throughout and describes the production processes and the thinking behind them. In his Foreword, BBC Executive Producer Guy Freeman states: "Working with the whole lighting team on such a special project was a real treat for me and a fantastic achievement for them, which the pages of this book give a remarkable insight into."

Lighting the Stage *Francis Reid 120pp* **£14.95** ISBN: 9781904031086
Lighting the Stage discusses the human relationships involved in lighting design – both between people, and between these people and technology. The book is written from a highly personal viewpoint and its 'thinking aloud' approach is one that Francis Reid has used in his writings over the past 30 years.

Miscellany of Lighting and Stagecraft *Michael Hall & Julie Harper 222pp* **£22.95** ISBN: 9781904031680
This title will help schools, colleges, amateurs, technicians and all those interested in practical theatre and performance to understand, in an entertaining and informative way, the key backstage skills. Within its pages, numerous professionals share their own special knowledge and expertise, interspersed with diversions of historic interest and anecdotes from those practising at the front line of the industry. As a result, much of the advice and skills set out have not previously been set in print. The editors' intention with this book is to provide a Miscellany that is not ordered or categorised in strict fashion, but rather encourages the reader to flick through or dip into it, finding nuggets of information and anecdotes to entertain, inspire and engender curiosity – also to invite further research or exploration and generally encourage people to enter the industry and find out for themselves.

Mr Phipps' Theatre *Mark Jones, John Pick 172pp* £17.95 ISBN: 9781904031383
Mark Jones and John Pick describe "The Sensational Story of Eastbourne's Royal Hippodrome" – formerly Eastbourne Theatre Royal. An intriguing narrative, the book sets the story against a unique social history of the town. Peter Longman, former director of The Theatres Trust, provides the Foreword.

Northen Lights *Michael Northen 256pp* **£17.95** ISBN: 9781904031666
Many books have been written by famous personalities in the theatre about their lives and work. However this is probably one of the first memoirs by someone who has spent his entire career behind scenes, and not in front of the footlights. As a lighting designer and as consultant to designers and directors, Michael Northen worked through an exciting period of fifty years of theatrical history from the late nineteen thirties in theatres in the UK and abroad, and on productions ranging from Shakespeare, opera and ballet to straight plays, pantomimes and cabaret. This is not a complicated technical text book, but is intended to give an insight into some of the 300 productions in which he had been involved and some of the directors, the designers and backstage staff he have worked with, viewed from a new angle.

Pages From Stages *Anthony Field 204pp* **£17.95** ISBN: 9781904031260
Anthony Field explores the changing style of theatres including interior design, exterior design, ticket and seat prices, and levels of service, while questioning whether the theatre still exists as a place of entertainment for regular theatre-goers.

People, Places, Performances *Remembered by Francis Reid 60pp* **£8.95**
ISBN: 9781904031765
In growing older, the Author has found that memories, rather than featuring the events, increasingly tend to focus on the people who caused them, the places where they happened and the performances that arose. So Francis Reid has used these categories in endeavouring to compile a brief history of the second half of the twentieth century.

Performing Arts Technical Training Handbook 2013/2014 *ed: John Offord 304pp*
£19.95 ISBN: 9781904031710
Published in association with the ABTT (Association of British Theatre Technicians), this important Handbook, now in its third edition, includes fully detailed and indexed entries describing courses on backstage crafts offered by over 100 universities and colleges across the UK. A completely new research project, with accompanying website, the title also includes articles with advice for those considering a career 'behind the scenes', together with contact information and descriptions of the major organisations involved with industry training – plus details of companies offering training within their own premises.

Practical Dimming *Nick Mobsby 364pp* **£22.95** ISBN: 97819040313444
This important and easy to read title covers the history of electrical and electronic dimming, how dimmers work, current dimmer types from around the world, planning of a dimming system, looking at new sine wave dimming technology and distributed dimming. Integration of dimming into different performance venues as well as the necessary supporting electrical systems are fully detailed. Significant levels of information are provided on the many different forms and costs of potential solutions as well as how to plan specific solutions. Architectural dimming for the likes of hotels, museums and shopping centres is included. Practical Dimming is a companion book to Practical DMX and is designed for all involved in the use, operation and design of dimming systems.

Practical DMX *Nick Mobsby 276pp* **£16.95** ISBN: 9781904031369
In this highly topical and important title the author details the principles of DMX, how to plan a network, how to choose equipment and cables, with data on products from around the world, and how to install DMX networks for shows and on a permanently installed basis. The easy style of the book and the helpful fault finding tips, together with a review of different DMX testing devices provide an ideal companion for all lighting technicians and system designers. An introduction to Ethernet and Canbus networks are provided as well as tips on analogue networks and protocol conversion. It also includes a chapter on Remote Device Management.

A Practical Guide to Health and Safety in the Entertainment Industry
Marco van Beek 120pp **£14.95** ISBN: 9781904031048
This book is designed to provide a practical approach to Health and Safety within the Live Entertainment and Event industry. It gives industry-pertinent examples, and seeks to break down the myths surrounding Health and Safety.

Production Management *Joe Aveline 134pp* **£17.95** ISBN: 9781904031109
Joe Aveline's book is an in-depth guide to the role of the Production Manager, and includes real-life practical examples and 'Aveline's Fables' – anecdotes of his experiences with real messages behind them.

Rigging for Entertainment: Regulations and Practice *Chris Higgs 156pp* **£19.95** ISBN: 9781904031215
Continuing where he left off with his highly successful An Introduction to Rigging in the Entertainment Industry, Chris Higgs' second title covers the regulations and use of equipment in greater detail.

Rock Solid Ethernet *Wayne Howell 304pp* **£23.95** ISBN: 9781904031697
Now in its third completely revised and reset edition, Rock Solid Ethernet is aimed specifically at specifiers, installers and users of entertainment industry systems, and will give the reader a thorough grounding in all aspects of computer networks, whatever industry they may work in. The inclusion of historical and technical 'sidebars' make for an enjoyable as well as an informative read.

Sixty Years of Light Work *Fred Bentham 450pp* **£26.95** ISBN: 9781904031079
This title is an autobiography of one of the great names behind the development of modern stage lighting equipment and techniques. It includes a complete facsimile of the famous Strand Electric Catalogue of May 1936 – a reference work in itself.

Sound for the Stage *Patrick Finelli 218pp* **£24.95** ISBN: 9781904031154
Patrick Finelli's thorough manual covering all aspects of live and recorded sound for performance is a complete training course for anyone interested in working in the field of stage sound, and is a must for any student of sound.

Stage Automation *Anton Woodward 128pp* **£12.95** ISBN: 9781904031567
The purpose of this book is to explain the stage automation techniques used in modern theatre to achieve some of the spectacular visual effects seen in recent years. The book is targeted at automation operators, production managers, theatre technicians, stage engineering machinery manufacturers and theatre engineering students. Topics are covered in sufficient detail to provide an insight into the thought processes that the stage automation engineer has to consider when designing a control system to control stage machinery in a modern theatre. The author has worked on many stage automation projects and developed the award-winning Impressario stage automation system.

Stage Lighting Design in Britain: The Emergence of the Lighting Designer, 1881-1950
Nigel Morgan 300pp **£17.95** ISBN: 9781904031345
This title sets out to ascertain the main course of events and the controlling factors that determined the emergence of the theatre lighting designer in Britain, starting with the introduction of incandescent electric light to the stage, and ending at the time of the first public lighting design credits around 1950. The book explores the practitioners, equipment, installations and techniques of lighting design.

Stage Lighting for Theatre Designers *Nigel Morgan 124pp* **£17.95**
ISBN: 9781904031192
This is an updated second edition of Nigel Morgan's popular book for students of theatre design – outlining all the techniques of stage lighting design.

Technical Marketing Techniques *David Brooks, Andy Collier, Steve Norman 160pp*
£24.95 ISBN: 9781904031031
Technical Marketing is a novel concept, defined and elaborated by the authors of this book, with business-to-business companies competing in fast developing technical product sectors.

Technical Standards for Places of Entertainment *ABTT 354pp A4* **£45.00**
ISBN: 9781904031703
Technical Standards for Places of Entertainment details the necessary physical standards required for entertainment venues. Known in the industry as the "Yellow Book" the latest completely revised edition was first published in June 2013.

Theatre Engineering and Stage Machinery *Toshiro Ogawa 332pp* **£30.00**
ISBN: 9781904031024
Theatre Engineering and Stage Machinery is a unique reference work covering every aspect of theatrical machinery and stage technology in global terms, and across the complete historical spectrum. Revised February 2007.

Theatre Lighting in the Age of Gas *Terence Rees 232pp* **£24.95**
ISBN: 9781904031178
Entertainment Technology Press has republished this valuable historic work previously produced by the Society for Theatre Research in 1978. Theatre Lighting in the Age of Gas investigates the technological and artistic achievements of theatre lighting engineers from the 1700s to the late Victorian period.

Theatre Space: A Rediscovery Reported *Francis Reid 238pp* **£19.95**
ISBN: 9781904031437
In the post-war world of the 1950s and 60s, the format of theatre space became a matter for a debate that aroused passions of an intensity unknown before or since. The proscenium arch was clearly identified as the enemy, accused of forming a barrier to disrupt the relations between the actor and audience. An uneasy fellow-traveller at the time, Francis Reid later recorded his impressions whilst enjoying performances or working in theatres old and new and this book is an important collection of his writings in various theatrical journals from

1969-2001 including his contribution to the Cambridge Guide to the Theatre in 1988. It reports some of the flavour of the period when theatre architecture was rediscovering its past in a search to establish its future.

The Theatres and Concert Halls of Fellner and Helmer *Michael Sell 246pp* **£23.95** ISBN: 9781904031772
This is the first British study of the works of the prolific Fellner and Helmer Atelier which was active from 1871-1914 during which time they produced over 80 theatre designs and are second in quantity only to Frank Matcham, to whom reference is made.
This period is one of great change as a number of serious theatre fires which included Nice and Vienna had the effect of the introduction of safety legislation which affected theatre design. This study seeks to show how Fellner and Helmer and Frank Matcham dealt with this increasing safety legislation, in particular the way in which safety was built into their new three part theatres equipped with iron stages, safety curtains, electricity and appropriate access and egress and, in the Vienna practice, how this was achieved across 13 countries.

Theatres of Achievement *John Higgins 302pp* **£29.95** ISBN: 9781904031376
John Higgins affectionately describes the history of 40 distinguished UK theatres in a personal tribute, each uniquely illustrated by the author. Completing each profile is colour photography by Adrian Eggleston.

Theatric Tourist *Francis Reid 220pp* **£19.95** ISBN: 9781904031468
Theatric Tourist is the delightful story of Francis Reid's visits across more than 50 years to theatres, theatre museums, performances and even movie theme parks. In his inimitable style, the author involves the reader within a personal experience of venues from the Legacy of Rome to theatres of the Renaissance and Eighteenth Century Baroque and the Gustavian Theatres of Stockholm. His performance experiences include Wagner in Beyreuth, the Pleasures of Tivoli and Wayang in Singapore. This is a 'must have' title for those who are as "incurably stagestruck" as the author.

Through the Viewfinder *Jeremy Hoare 276pp* **£21.95** ISBN:: 9781904031574
Do you want to be a top television cameraman? Well this is going to help!
Through the Viewfinder is aimed at media students wanting to be top professional television cameramen – but it will also be of interest to anyone who wants to know what goes on behind the cameras that bring so much into our homes.
The author takes his own opinionated look at how to operate a television camera based on 23 years' experience looking through many viewfinders for a major ITV network company. Based on interviews with people he has worked with, all leaders in the profession, the book is based on their views and opinions and is a highly revealing portrait of what happens behind the scenes in television production from a cameraman's point of view.

Walt Disney Concert Hall – The Backstage Story *Patricia MacKay & Richard Pilbrow 250pp* **£28.95** ISBN: 9781904031239
Spanning the 16-year history of the design and construction of the Walt Disney Concert Hall, this book provides a fresh and detailed behind the scenes story of the design and

technology from a variety of viewpoints. This is the first book to reveal the "process" of the design of a concert hall.

Yesterday's Lights – A Revolution Reported   *Francis Reid 352pp*   **£26.95**
ISBN: 9781904031321
Set to help new generations to be aware of where the art and science of theatre lighting is coming from – and stimulate a nostalgia trip for those who lived through the period, Francis Reid's latest book has over 350 pages dedicated to the task, covering the 'revolution' from the fifties through to the present day. Although this is a highly personal account of the development of lighting design and technology and he admits that there are 'gaps', you'd be hard put to find anything of significance missing.

Go to www.etbooks.co.uk for full details of above titles and secure online ordering facilities. Most books also available for Kindle.